W E I R D
AND
WONDERFUL

INSECTS

SUE HADDEN

Thomson Learning
New York

WEIRD AND WONDERFUL

FISH
FROGS & TOADS
INSECTS
SNAKES

Cover: A mantis nymph mimicking a flower.

Editor: Geraldine Purcell
Designer: Bruce Low

First published in the United States in 1993 by
Thomson Learning; 115 Fifth Avenue; New York, NY 10003

First published in 1991 by Wayland (Publishers) Limited
61 Western Road, Hove, East Sussex, BN3 IJD, England

Library of Congress Cataloging-in-Publication Data

Hadden, Sue.
   Insects / by Sue Hadden.
      p. cm. — (Weird and wonderful)
   Originally published: Hove, East Sussex, England : Wayland, c1991.
   Includes bibliographical references (p.) and index.
   Summary: Examines the habitats and characteristics of various
insects, including the ladybug, water measurer, and stag beetle.
   ISBN 1-56847-009-6
   1. Insects—Juvenile literature. [1. Insects.] I. Title.
II. Series.
QL467.2.H33 1993
   595.7—dc20   91-15625

Printed in the United States of America

CONTENTS

1.   Large and small

There are at least 750,000 different **species** of insect in the world. Some scientists think there may be over 10 million species. With so many different kinds of insects, it is not surprising that they come in all shapes and sizes.

You would soon notice a goliath beetle if it landed close to you! This flying, giant African beetle is the heaviest insect in the world, weighing about 1/4 lb. Goliath beetles are very long too, about 6 inches. Such large flying insects may look frightening, but they are harmless fruit-eating insects.

Some insects are so small that you need a magnifying glass to see them clearly. Springtails are tiny insects, often 1/25 inch or less. Different kinds of springtails and other tiny insects live in many places. Look carefully in the soil or among leaf litter, around ponds, or at the seashore and you may spot one of these mini-beasts.

Below This goliath beetle is almost as big as the banana it is eating.

Right A group of freshwater springtails on the surface of a pond.

2. Odd bodies and strange faces

This violin beetle from the forests of Indonesia is certainly one of the more oddly-shaped insects. Its body flaps make it look like a violin, but the flaps really help the beetle to blend in with the pattern of a tree fungus. Although the violin beetle has a very odd-looking body, it has the same features that most insects have. It has six legs, a pair of **antennae**, and a body divided into three sections: the head, the **thorax,** and the **abdomen**.

Left Its long neck and round body have given the violin beetle its name.

The lantern fly from southeast Asia and South America has a very strange face that bulges out like a huge false head. No one is sure why the fly has a face shaped like this, but it is probably to scare away its enemies. Lantern flies may look fierce, but they are harmless and feed on sap (juices) from plants and trees. They are called lantern flies because people used to believe that the large, false head glowed in the dark, like a lantern, but this is not true.

Below Its odd-looking head makes the lantern fly look very scary.

3. Changing shape

Insects hatch from eggs, and then almost all go through a series of amazing body-changing stages, called **metamorphosis**. After hatching, an insect usually becomes a **larva** and then a **pupa** before reaching its final adult body form.

A ladybug, for example, hatches out of an egg in early summer. The larva eats as much as it can, for it needs plenty of energy to turn into a pupa. Its body slowly changes shape within its tight pupal skin. Months later, the larva comes out of the pupa as an adult ladybug, with wings, ready to fly.

Some insects, such as the damselfly, have young that look much like the adult, only smaller. The young (called nymphs) live in ponds. The nymph sheds its skin each time its body gets bigger. Gradually, it grows wings, and its body and legs grow longer.

When it is ready to become an adult, the nymph crawls out of the pond onto a plant stalk. There the nymph's skin splits, and a new damselfly emerges. This process is called "incomplete metamorphosis."

Below When ladybugs come out of their pupal skin, they do not have spots.

Right A damselfly pushing itself out of its old nymph skin.

4.   On the move

Some insects have amazing ways of traveling, whether in the air or over water.

A cockchafer beetle has to work hard to lift its heavy body and sturdy legs off the ground. To get airborne, the chafer must pump plenty of air into air sacs (pockets) in its body.

Cockchafers are noisy, clumsy flyers and on fine summer evenings they often fly into people's homes and zoom around the lights. But, although they keep bumping into objects and falling to the floor, these heavyweight beetles rarely hurt themselves.

Left A cockchafer in flight. You can see its clear wings and wing cases.

The water measurer walks around on the surfaces of ponds and lakes. How does it do this without sinking? Well, this insect is very lightweight. It uses its long legs to spread its weight evenly across the water surface. Also, the water measurer is supported by the thin but very strong film formed by the water surface. (This is called surface tension.) The water measurer rests on the surface, waiting for a tiny insect or insect larva to pass by in the pond. The water measurer then moves across the water and quickly stabs its **prey** with its sharp mouthparts.

Below A water measurer resting on the surface of a pond.

5. Home sweet home

Insects live in a wide variety of places—underground, in trees or in and around water.

Some, such as the water scorpion, spend their entire lives under water. The water scorpion stays below the surface and when another insect or a small fish passes by, the water scorpion seizes it with pincerlike front legs. These insects can stay under water because they have a special breathing tube, like a snorkel. It sticks out of the water and brings air down to the water scorpion in the pond.

Below A larva is being used to help the weaver ants glue a nest together.

Weaver ants have an unusual way of making a home—they sew one! The ants live in the **tropical** forests of Africa, Southeast Asia and Australia, so they can find plenty of leaves. First of all a line of worker ants pulls two leaves together. Then other worker ants sew up the leaves with sticky strands of silk produced from ant larvae. Each worker ant holds a larva in its jaws and moves the larva from one side to the other, like someone using a needle and thread. The finished nest is a snug ball of leaves.

Right You can see the water scorpion's air tube reaching to the water's surface.

6. Food stores

Some insects live in harsh climates. Many of them must develop special ways of getting food and water.

Honeypot ants live in many dry areas of the world, including the Australian desert and the southwestern United States. During the very short rainy season, the ants feed on nectar from desert flowers. But in the long dry season, the flowers cannot grow. To avoid starving, the ants survive by using some of the worker ants as honey stores. In the rainy season, these "storage ants" are constantly fed with nectar and water until their abdomens swell up like balloons! They store enough honey to feed the whole ant colony until the flowers bloom again.

Darkling beetles live in the hot, dry Namib desert of Southern Africa. The only moisture there comes from mist that drifts in off the Atlantic Ocean. The mist is too fine to drink but it slowly **condenses** into water droplets when it touches the darkling beetle's body. Then the beetle tilts up its body and the droplets run down the grooves on its back, into its thirsty mouth.

Left This honeypot ant is used as a store for honey for the ant colony.

Below A darkling beetle in its dry desert home.

7. Insect assassins

Many insects hunt other insects for food. They have some interesting ways of catching their prey.

One of the fiercest hunters is the praying mantis. This strange-looking insect lives in warm parts of the world, especially tropical countries. The mantis waits under a flower or a leaf, keeping very still, so that it is hard to see. When an insect comes to feed, the mantis seizes it with its razor-sharp claws. Its victim cannot escape and will be eaten alive.

Assassin bugs are also fierce insect-eaters. They are armed with sharp, piercing mouthparts. Once the assassin bug has seized an insect in its forelegs, it injects poison to stop its prey from struggling. Then the bug uses its sharp mouth-tube to suck the blood out of its prey.

Below An assassin bug, from Central America, feeding on its prey.

Right Mantises are fierce hunters and sometimes they even eat each other.

8. Hide and seek

Many insects are **camouflaged** either to avoid being eaten or to hide so that they can catch their prey by surprise.

Flower mantises have white, pink, or green colors to blend in with tropical flowers. Some have legs shaped like flat, flower petals. When a flower mantis sits still on the type of flower it matches in color, the mantis is perfectly disguised. Any insect or small bird coming to visit the beautiful flower for nectar has a nasty surprise in store!

Cleverly disguised insects called thorn bugs use camouflage to protect themselves from **predators**. They stay as a group, all facing in one direction, on a plant's stem. The bugs keep very still, so that predators, such as birds, are fooled into thinking that they are just thorns on a stem. In this way the thorn bugs usually avoid being eaten.

Left When hunting, this flower mantis hides among white tropical flowers.

Below These thorn bugs look like rows of thorns on a stem.

9.   Leave me alone!

Insects often use color and patterns to warn predators to keep away. Nature uses three colors as warning signals: red, yellow, and black. Birds and other animals have learned that insects of these colors are poisonous, or at least taste unpleasant.

The **caterpillars** of the cinnabar moth are poisonous, and their yellow and black stripes warn birds not to eat them. Adult cinnabar moths have red and black wings, showing that they too are poisonous. Warning colors can also be seen in insects with powerful stings, such as bees and wasps that have yellow and black stripes.

Patterns on insects also serve a purpose. The io moth from the United States has a pair of large spots on its hind wings. They look just like staring eyes. The moth does not usually show "eyes" when it is resting. But if a bird or other predator comes near, the io moth flashes its eyespots and flies off. The big eyes may frighten the bird or confuse it for a moment, giving the moth time to escape.

Below An io moth shows its large eye spots to warn off an enemy.

Right Poisonous cinnabar moths are red and black in color.

10. Pretenders

Not all insects are what they seem. The hornet moth has a very useful disguise. With its yellow stripes and clear, narrow wings, the moth fools its predators into believing it is a dangerous hornet. The only clues that give the moth away are that it has thicker legs than a wasp, and it has the antennae of a moth. But birds are none the wiser and most predators leave this moth alone, so it enjoys a peaceful life.

Left This "hornet" would not sting you because it is really a hornet moth.

Birds keep well away from some kinds of ants, which can squirt acid from their tails. So a type of harmless tropical treehopper has developed a fantastic disguise as an ant. Its abdomen, legs, and wings all blend in with the leaf it sits on. From a distance, only the black ant marking on its thorax shows up. Predators avoid the "ant," and the treehopper is safe. What a brilliant trick for an unarmed bug!

Below A predator would be fooled by this treehopper's disguise as an ant.

11. Fierce and fearless

Caterpillars usually rely on good camouflage or on sharp spines to protect them from being eaten. But one caterpillar defends itself in an amazing way.

The fierce-looking puss moth caterpillar rears up at an enemy, lashing out with its whiplike tail streamers. To look more frightening, the caterpillar draws in its head to show a bright red patch and false eyes. Sometimes it squirts strong acid at the enemy. This startling display scares away most predators. Afterward, when it is no longer in danger, the caterpillar returns to looking quite normal and harmless.

Male stag beetles fight over the right to **mate** with a female. They have a wrestling match using their huge, powerful jaws, which look like a pair of antlers, as weapons. A large male stag beetle can easily throw another male around, gripping him in pincerlike jaws. The loser gets thrown to the ground. Because of his strength, the winner of the battle is more likely to attract the female to mate with him.

Below Two male stag beetles in an impressive wrestling match.

Right A puss moth caterpillar looks very fierce when in its warning display.

12. Courtship signals

Colors are used by many insects during **courtship** to attract a mate.

Most moths fly and mate at night and therefore tend not to be so colorful. But one of the most beautiful and colorful moths in the world is the *Urania leilus* moth from South America. It flies during the day, so it has bright colors to attract a mate. The beautiful colors on the wings are produced by scales, which catch the sunlight as the moth flies. A mate will be able to see these shimmering colors and will be attracted to the moth.

Male and female glowworms attract each other at night with flashes of bright green light. The light comes from a special **organ** in the tail. A male glowworm follows the much brighter flashes sent out by a female, until he finds her and then mates with her. Glowworms are not really worms, as you might think from the name, but members of the beetle family.

Left A glowworm flashing light from its tail is signaling that it is ready to mate.

Below This daytime flying moth has shimmering colors to attract a mate.

13. Parasites and partners

Poisonous tarantula spiders have little to fear from insects, except for the tarantula hawk wasp. The female hawk wasp attacks the dangerous tarantula with a vicious sting. When she has managed to sting the spider, it is **paralyzed**. While the tarantula cannot move, the female hawk wasp drags it into a burrow and lays an egg on it.

Later, the egg will hatch into a wasp larva and it will begin to eat the paralyzed tarantula. The spider cannot do anything about this, and it is eaten alive. The wasp larva is a **parasite**, living off the spider and giving it nothing in return.

Sometimes two very different insect species can live together and each gain some reward. For example, ants are known to look after a group of aphids. The aphids produce a delicious sweet liquid called honeydew, which the ants like to feed on. So the ants "milk" the honeydew from the aphids. As a kind of payment for this food source, the ants help to protect the aphids from predators, such as ladybugs.

Below A tarantula hawk wasp has caught its victim and will soon lay an egg on the spider.

Right An ant drinking honeydew from some aphids. Their partnership works well.

GLOSSARY

Abdomen The end part of an insect's body. Inside are its heart, digestive system, and organs for producing young.

Antennae The pair of feelers on an insect's head.

Camouflaged Colored or patterned to blend in with the background.

Caterpillar The pupal stage of a butterfly or moth.

Colony A group of insects living and working together.

Condenses Changes from water vapor (mist or steam) into water droplets.

Courtship The time when males and females of a species attract each other before they mate.

Larva The first stage of most insects after they hatch from the egg.

Mating The act that males and females of a species perform in order to reproduce.

Metamorphosis The series of changes that an insect goes through in developing from a larva to an adult.

Nectar The sugary substance produced by flowers.

Organ A part of the body, such as the heart, that performs a particular function.

Paralyzed Unable to move.

Parasite An animal (often an insect) that lives and feeds on another animal.

Predators Animals that hunt other animals for food.

Prey An animal that is hunted and eaten by another animal.

Pupa The stage in an insect's life when the larva slowly changes into the adult insect. The pupa seems to be resting in a tight skin, but in fact all kinds of changes are happening to its body.

Species A particular kind of animal that is different from all other kinds. Only members of the same species can mate and produce young.

Thorax The middle part of an insect's body, behind its head. The three pairs of legs and the wings are attached to the thorax.

Tropical The very warm parts of the earth, near the equator, that lie between the two imaginary lines around the earth that we call the Tropic of Cancer and the Tropic of Capricorn.

FURTHER READING

Backyard Insects, by Millicent Selsam and Ronald Goor (Scholastic, 1988)

Extinct Insects, by Philip Steele (Franklin Watts, 1992)

How Do Ants Know When You're Having a Picnic? And Other Questions Kids Ask about Insects & Other Crawly Things, by Joanne Settel and Nancy Baggett (Atheneum, 1986)

Insects. Eyewitness Explorers (Dorling Kindersley, 1992)

Insects & Their Relatives, by Maurice Burton (Facts on File, 1984)

Poisonous Insects, by Lionel Bender. First Sight (Gloucester Press, 1988)

Picture Acknowledgments

Ardea London Ltd/I. R. Beames 25, J. Mason 22; Bruce Coleman Ltd/J. & D. Bartlett 4, J. Burton 8, A. Compst 12, K. Taylor 10, 11, 15, 21; Frank Lane Pictures/B. Borrell 17, Hoflinger 29; NHPA/A. Bannister COVER, S. Dalton 19, 24, O. Rogge 14, M. W. F. Tweedie 27; Oxford Scientific Films Ltd/G. I. Bernard 5, R. Blythe 26, J. A. L. Cooke 23, P. Devries 7, 16, M. Fogden 28, R. Jackman 13, Mantis Wildlife Films 6, J. Robinson 20; Papilio/18; Planet Earth Pictures/W. Harris 9.

INDEX

Numbers in **bold** indicate photographs.